Original title:
The Things We Carry

Copyright © 2024 Swan Charm
All rights reserved.

Author: Kene Elistrand
ISBN HARDBACK: 978-9916-89-939-7
ISBN PAPERBACK: 978-9916-89-940-3
ISBN EBOOK: 978-9916-89-941-0

Soul's Baggage

In shadows deep, our burdens grow,
Each weight we carry, a tale to sow.
With faith as light, we journey on,
Releasing chains, till night is gone.

The paths we tread, in grace we find,
Old echoes whisper, love unconfined.
With every sigh, we shed the past,
Embracing joy, our hearts steadfast.

Heartbeats of the Past

Within the chambers, memories dwell,
Each heartbeat echoes, a sacred bell.
Stories linger, woven so tight,
In shadows' dance, we seek the light.

The whispers of souls, both near and far,
Guide our steps, like a guiding star.
In prayer we listen, to lessons true,
Hearts pulse in rhythm, to all we knew.

Reflections on the Journey

Waves of faith upon the shore,
Each step we take, we long for more.
In every trial, a lesson learned,
Through winding roads, our spirits yearned.

With open hearts, we rise and fall,
In unity's grace, we answer the call.
The tapestry of life unfolds wide,
In love's embrace, we choose to bide.

Sacred Fragments

In pieces scattered, yet whole we stand,
Each fragment precious, held in His hand.
Through trials faced, we find our way,
In shattered glass, a brighter day.

With faith as glue, our souls align,
Mending the heart, a design divine.
We rise from ashes, restored and free,
In sacred fragments, we find the key.

The Beauty of Battered Souls

In shadows deep where sorrow dwells,
The battered soul, a tale it tells.
With faith like flowers in the rain,
They find the light beyond the pain.

Each scar a symbol, each tear a prayer,
A heart laid bare, the weight they bear.
In brokenness, the spirit soars,
A silent strength that heals and restores.

For in the dark, His love unfolds,
A canvas rich with hues of gold.
The weary find their moments bright,
Transcending pain, embracing light.

The journey hard, yet worth the climb,
In every ache a slice of time.
The battered souls, they stand so tall,
In grace they rise, despite the fall.

Legacy of the Anxious Heart

In whispered prayers beneath the night,
Anxious hearts seek solace, light.
With trembling hands and hopeful sighs,
They quest for peace beneath the skies.

Each worry woven into fate,
A tapestry of love and weight.
In fear's embrace, they learn to trust,
To rise above, to fight, to thrust.

The legacy of doubt and grace,
Leaves woven paths for hope to trace.
In faith restored, their spirits mend,
The anxious heart will find a friend.

For every tear that falls in prayer,
Transforms the heart with love to share.
Legacy blooms in every heart's ache,
To find the peace that will not break.

Traces of Sanctity in Our Steps

With each footfall upon this earth,
We leave behind a tale of worth.
In simple acts and love displayed,
Sanctity lingers where we've prayed.

The quiet moments, a gentle sway,
In service found, we light the way.
Through trials faced and burdens shared,
In every step, a heart repaired.

The traces left, like whispers soft,
Echo in skies and drift aloft.
In kindness sown, in truth embraced,
The sacred paths in life we traced.

Together bound by faith and grace,
We walk in love, a sacred space.
Each journey blessed by what we give,
In that, our souls will truly live.

Stones of Remembrance

In the quiet of the night,
Stones whisper tales of old,
Markers of faith and fight,
Their wisdom, a treasure untold.

Upon the path we tread,
Echoes of voices remain,
Stories of the faithful led,
Through hope and through pain.

Each stone holds a prayer,
A cry of the heart and soul,
A promise of love laid bare,
In the hands of the whole.

With each step we do take,
Their strength becomes ours to know,
In shadows, they gently wake,
Reminding us how to grow.

Let them guide our way,
Through the darkness and light,
In the dawn of each day,
Stones of remembrance shine bright.

Longing and Light

In the depth of my yearning,
There shines a flicker divine,
Hope in the quiet burning,
A whisper that says, 'You're mine.'

Through valleys of shadows cast,
The path seems lonely, yet warm,
Each moment a sacred blast,
Of love that can weather the storm.

With hearts raised to the sky,
We seek what is pure and right,
Our souls, like birds, they fly,
Towards eternal, sacred light.

In the dance of the flames,
We find solace and grace,
Every longing, it claims,
A journey to His embrace.

As dawn breaks anew,
With promises to keep,
In each breath, there's a view,
Of love that runs deep.

Stones of Remembrance

In the quiet of the night,
Stones whisper tales of old,
Markers of faith and fight,
Their wisdom, a treasure untold.

Upon the path we tread,
Echoes of voices remain,
Stories of the faithful led,
Through hope and through pain.

Each stone holds a prayer,
A cry of the heart and soul,
A promise of love laid bare,
In the hands of the whole.

With each step we do take,
Their strength becomes ours to know,
In shadows, they gently wake,
Reminding us how to grow.

Let them guide our way,
Through the darkness and light,
In the dawn of each day,
Stones of remembrance shine bright.

Longing and Light

In the depth of my yearning,
There shines a flicker divine,
Hope in the quiet burning,
A whisper that says, 'You're mine.'

Through valleys of shadows cast,
The path seems lonely, yet warm,
Each moment a sacred blast,
Of love that can weather the storm.

With hearts raised to the sky,
We seek what is pure and right,
Our souls, like birds, they fly,
Towards eternal, sacred light.

In the dance of the flames,
We find solace and grace,
Every longing, it claims,
A journey to His embrace.

As dawn breaks anew,
With promises to keep,
In each breath, there's a view,
Of love that runs deep.

Pilgrim's Yoke

Beneath the weight we bear,
A yoke made of faith and trust,
Each step a silent prayer,
In Him we find our just.

Travelers on this road,
With burdens marked by pain,
Yet the path gently goad,
Towards joy found in rain.

We walk as one, united,
In purpose, grace and song,
With hearts ever ignited,
Where we know we belong.

With every trial faced,
The yoke draws us near,
In His love, we're embraced,
Together, casting fear.

So we carry this load,
In the light of His face,
On this sacred road,
We find our resting place.

Honoring the Weight

In the silence we gather,
To honor the weight we hold,
Each life, a sacred patter,
With stories, rich and bold.

Through trials we emerge,
Our burdens shared with grace,
In unity, we surge,
Finding strength in this place.

The sacred ties that bind,
With love forged in the fire,
In hardships, peace we find,
As we rise, we aspire.

Each tear that we have shed,
Marks the path to our light,
Moving forward, well-led,
In the glow of the night.

Let us honor this weight,
As a gift to our kin,
In each moment, innate,
Lies the courage within.

Tapestries of Trials

In shadows deep where fears abide,
We weave our dreams, let faith be our guide.
Each thread a story, a challenge faced,
In the loom of life, our strength is laced.

With hands so weary, but hearts aflame,
We rise to meet the calling, the same.
In every struggle, a lesson we find,
A tapestry rich, by grace intertwined.

Quiet Carriers

Beneath the sky, so vast and wide,
Whispered truths in silence reside.
The simple souls on paths unknown,
Carry their burdens, yet never alone.

With gentle hearts, they sow the seeds,
Of love and kindness in quiet deeds.
Their light will shine in darkest night,
Guiding the weary toward the light.

Clouds of Reverie

Upon the hill where soft winds blow,
Dreams take flight, like clouds that flow.
In realms of peace our spirits soar,
Finding solace on heaven's shore.

Each thought a feather, light and bright,
Carried on wings of heavenly sight.
In this embrace, our worries cease,
In clouds of reverie, we find our peace.

Sacred Loads

We journey forth with sacred loads,
In every heart, a path that codes.
The weight of love, the pain we bear,
Turns trials into blessings rare.

With every step, our spirits grow,
In faith's embrace, we come to know.
That burdens shared bring strength anew,
In sacred loads, we rise as true.

Grief's Gravitational Pull

In shadows deep, our sorrow we bear,
A weight that lingers, fills the air.
Yet through the tears, a light remains bright,
Hope's gentle whisper, guiding the night.

In every loss, a lesson profound,
Life's fleeting touch, in silence found.
We clasp the memories, hold them tight,
For love persists, a beacon of light.

Though grief may anchor, we rise anew,
Faith's tender promise will see us through.
Each moment bestowed, we cherish the grace,
In pain, we find our rightful place.

As seasons change, the heart will mend,
From ashes, we blossom, we transcend.
With every heartbeat, we learn to cope,
In grief's embrace, we nurture hope.

Testament of the Indomitable Spirit

Within the soul, a fire ignites,
A strength unyielding, shining bright.
Though trials come, and shadows fall,
We rise as one, we heed the call.

For in the struggle, our essence defined,
A tapestry woven, hearts intertwined.
With every challenge, resolve we attain,
A testament forged in joy and pain.

Guided by faith, we stand unafraid,
In unity's power, foundations laid.
The spirit within, relentless and true,
Emerges from darkness, begins anew.

With every heartbeat, we march along,
Together we sing our resilient song.
Each moment a gift, each breath a prayer,
In the face of strife, we meet despair.

Against the tempest, with courage we strive,
In the depths of turmoil, we learn to thrive.
A legacy rich, as we journey forth,
The indomitable spirit, proving our worth.

Celestial Echoes of Earthly Strain

In the stillness, echoes resound,
The cries of the weary, searching ground.
Stars above, with wisdom to share,
If we but listen, find solace there.

Nature whispers softly, a balm to the soul,
Each rustling leaf, reminding us whole.
Through storms that rage, and skies that weep,
Celestial bodies in silence keep.

Within the chaos, a rhythm we sense,
In every heartache, an unseen fence.
Bound by the weight of earthly despair,
Yet lifted by faith, in cosmic air.

Embracing the struggle, we rise and bend,
Finding beauty in paths that don't end.
The universe sings, a haunting refrain,
Celestial echoes amidst earthly strain.

Harmony in the Heart's Heaviness

In shadows cast by sorrow's loom,
A melody whispers, dispelling gloom.
Within the heart, heaviness resides,
Yet harmony hums, as love abides.

Like rivers flowing, emotions entwine,
Pain and joy dancing, both divine.
For in each heartbeat, the struggle sings,
Balancing burdens with what hope brings.

Through trials faced, we learn to embrace,
The light in the dark, a warm grace.
In every tear, a story we tell,
In unity's strength, we rise from the well.

Together we find, in shared despair,
A harmony woven with tender care.
From heaviness birthed, a song of the soul,
In love's sweet embrace, we become whole.

Reverent Remnants

In shadows deep, where silence reigns,
The echoes whisper of sacred gains.
Through trials faced, the spirit weaves,
A tapestry of hope that never leaves.

Upon the altar, a flickering light,
Guiding lost hearts through the night.
With humble prayers, in faith we stand,
Embracing grace with open hands.

A sacred bond, through prayer we grow,
In reverent groves, the ancients know.
Their wisdom shines, like stars above,
A chain unbroken, woven in love.

Each moment cherished, a treasure rare,
In every heartbeat, we find our prayer.
The remnants speak of truths divine,
In every soul, a spark that shines.

Together we walk, though paths may part,
With reverent remnants etched in heart.
In sacred peace, our spirits soar,
With faith as wings, forevermore.

Covenant Carried

In the stillness, we gather near,
Voices rise, a chorus clear.
A covenant drawn, beneath the sky,
In sacred trust, our spirits fly.

Through storms and trials, we bear the weight,
Holding fast to love, our faithful state.
With open hearts, we share our plight,
In every dawn, we seek the light.

The ancient words, like rivers flow,
Binding us close, where blessings grow.
Through joy and sorrow, hand in hand,
In unity, our hopes expand.

Each promise made, a sacred thread,
We weave our lives, where angels tread.
In quiet moments, the truth we find,
A covenant carried, eternally kind.

As seasons change, and ages pass,
Our faith endures, like polished glass.
In each embrace, the world transforms,
With love's warm light, our spirit warms.

Offering from the Depths

From silent depths, a call resounds,
In darkest hours, salvation found.
With each breath, a gift we share,
An offering born from deepest care.

In the still waters, a wisdom flows,
A sacred heart that gently grows.
With open hands, we give our all,
In every stumble, we rise tall.

Through trials faced and battles fought,
We find the grace that love has wrought.
From ashes rise, our spirits free,
An offering whispered, eternally.

Each tear a token, each laugh a song,
In tender moments, we all belong.
In depths uncharted, the light appears,
An offering from darkness, washed in tears.

With gratitude deep, we fill the cup,
In every heartbeat, we lift it up.
A radiant glow, in truth we see,
The offering from depths, pure as can be.

Journey of Souls

Upon the road where shadows play,
The journey starts at dawn's first ray.
With footprints left on sacred ground,
In every heart, a love profound.

Through valleys low and mountains high,
Our spirits soar beyond the sky.
In every whisper, a guiding star,
A journey mapped, though near and far.

As rivers flow, so do we roam,
In search of light, we find our home.
With every breath, the story grows,
A journey of souls that forever flows.

In gentle winds, we hear the call,
A harmony that unites us all.
Through laughter shared and burdens borne,
In journey's weave, new paths are sworn.

With every dawn, a chapter turns,
The flame of faith within us burns.
Together bound, the love we know,
In the journey of souls, we eternally glow.

Divine Encounters

In stillness, the spirit gleams,
Whispers in the sacred light,
Hearts open to endless dreams,
Guided by love's gentle might.

Angels dance on stones of grace,
Echoes of a holy song,
In the silence, find His face,
Where the lost and found belong.

In shadows, His light ignites,
Casting doubts into the sea,
With faith, we ascend the heights,
In unity, we are free.

Each prayer a fragrant offering,
Lifted high on wings of hope,
In the joy of discovering,
Together, we learn to cope.

Here in His divine embrace,
We are woven, thread by thread,
In each heart, we find our place,
A tapestry of love spread.

Holy Journeys

We wander roads of ancient times,
Seeking signs along the way,
In every heartbeat, sacred rhymes,
Echo through the night and day.

The stars align in destiny,
Guiding steps with gentle grace,
In every choice, His symphony,
In every dream, His soft embrace.

With open hearts, we walk this path,
Through trials, joys, and lessons learned,
In moments blessed by holy wrath,
An enduring fire, brightly burned.

Our burdens lightened by His love,
We share the weight we cannot bear,
Through faith, we rise to realms above,
In His presence, free from care.

Each journey brings a newfound sight,
A glimpse of what must surely be,
In purity, we find our light,
As we walk on, eternally.

Souls in Transit

Drifting through this earthly realm,
We search for solace, seek to find,
In every heart, a blessed helm,
Guiding us toward the divine.

Between the worlds, we ebb and flow,
Carrying dreams through night and day,
In each connection, love does grow,
As sacred truths show us the way.

In whispers shared, our spirits soar,
A bond of grace, unseen yet known,
In every laugh, a holy door,
Where the love of God is shown.

In trials faced, we learn to trust,
That each moment's grounded in grace,
For in His love, we must adjust,
And maintain our chosen pace.

Through transient lives, we hold the thread,
Of mercy, kindness, shining bright,
In unity, we are all led,
As spirits dance in holy light.

Blessings in the Balance

In the stillness of the dawn,
We find our peace, our sacred space,
With every thought, the night withdrawn,
Embracing love's eternal grace.

With gratitude, we count the stars,
Each twinkle a divine caress,
In life's abundance, near and far,
We gather blessings, we are blessed.

Between each trial lies a gift,
A lesson wrapped in wisdom's fold,
As we rise and ever uplift,
Through faith, our stories are told.

In humble hearts, content we stand,
Finding joy in every chance,
With open arms, we hold His hand,
In life's fleeting, sacred dance.

As seasons change, we learn to see,
The balance of love and light creates,
In every moment, we are free,
For blessings lie at heaven's gates.

Walks of Reverence

In quiet woods, the shadows play,
With whispered prayers, we find our way.
Each leaf, a testament to grace,
In nature's arms, we seek His face.

The river flows, a sacred song,
It carries hopes, where hearts belong.
In every stone, a story stays,
Of love and peace in life's own maze.

Upon the hill, we stand in awe,
Beneath the sky, we see His law.
The stars above, they gently guide,
In faith, we walk, with Him our stride.

Heavenly Burdens

Upon our backs, the weight we bear,
Yet in each trial, we find His care.
With heavy hearts, we lift our eyes,
To clouds of hope that fill the skies.

The dawn breaks soft, a sign of love,
Reminding us of grace above.
Each tear we shed, a prayer set free,
In every struggle, He's there, we see.

We carry faith, like golden chains,
Through stormy nights and hopeful plains.
With every step, we learn to trust,
In Him alone, we find our must.

Pathways of the Spirit

On winding roads, where spirits soar,
We seek the light, forevermore.
Each step we take, a dance divine,
With every heartbeat, His love aligns.

In sacred dreams, our souls ignite,
We chase the stars, through endless night.
With open hearts, we breathe His grace,
Each moment shared, a warm embrace.

Through whispered winds, His guidance flows,
In every heart, His mercy grows.
Together we walk, on paths unknown,
In unity, we find our home.

Weight of Wisdom

In silent thoughts, the wise ones tread,
With ancient truths, the spirit fed.
Each lesson learned, a beacon bright,
Illuminating the darkest night.

With every age, the stories blend,
In shared laughter, we find a friend.
The wisdom flows like rivers deep,
In quiet moments, our secrets keep.

Through trials faced, we gain our sight,
In humble hearts, the glow of light.
We wear our burdens with gentle grace,
For in His presence, we find our place.

Pilgrims' Packs

With humble hearts, we tread this way,
Bearing our burdens of the day.
Each step we take in faith we find,
A path of light for weary mind.

In woven packs, our hopes reside,
Treasured dreams, the soul's true guide.
We carry forth the love we seek,
And find our strength in words we speak.

Through ancient trails, our spirits soar,
In unity, we long for more.
With every mile, a lesson learned,
For every gift, the heart has yearned.

Upon the road, kindness avows,
As gentle breezes bless our vows.
In unity, we lift each voice,
In praise and song, we make our choice.

So let us walk, the night may fall,
The stars will shine, our spirits call.
Each pilgrim's pack a tale to tell,
Of love and grace, we carry well.

Silent Echoes

In quiet prayer, the spirit sighs,
A whisper lost in twilight skies.
Echoes linger, soft and near,
Faith finds strength in silent fear.

The world may rush, but still we stand,
United by a stronger hand.
In silence, hearts begin to stir,
Amidst the chaos, we are sure.

Each moment held, a sacred trust,
In hope we dwell, in grace we must.
The echoes call, they guide our way,
In sacred space, we learn to pray.

When shadows loom and doubts arise,
In silent echoes, love replies.
A guiding light, within we seek,
In gentle hush, the brave grow meek.

So let us listen, hearts attune,
To whispers shared beneath the moon.
In silent grace, our lives align,
With every echo, souls entwine.

Offerings of the Spirit

We gather here with open hands,
To share the hope that love demands.
In sacred ritual, we bestow,
The gifts of heart that only grow.

Each offering laid at love's great feet,
A token sweet, a chance to meet.
In unity, our spirits rise,
Transcending pain, beneath the skies.

With gratitude, we share our pain,
Turning sadness into gain.
For every tear, a story told,
In spirit's warmth, we find our gold.

Together, bound by heavenly ties,
We lift our voices to the skies.
In offerings pure, our lives transform,
Through faith and love, our hearts grow warm.

So let us give, let kindness flow,
In humble hearts, our blessings grow.
For in this sharing, souls connect,
In offerings true, we find respect.

The Weight of Grace

Upon our shoulders lies the weight,
Of grace that flows and heals our fate.
Each burden borne with reverent care,
In love's embrace, we learn to share.

The trials faced, we rise anew,
In every challenge, we break through.
With every step, the heart expands,
In faith's embrace, the spirit stands.

The weight of grace, a heavy crown,
Yet lifts us high, never down.
In gratitude, we find our way,
Through darkest nights to brightest day.

So let us wear this mantle bright,
With open hearts to spread the light.
For in the weight of grace we find,
True freedom's path, both bold and kind.

Together we'll bear what's meant to be,
In every heart, a symphony.
The weight of grace, a blessed call,
In unity, we rise, we fall.

Shadows of Reverence

In the quiet night, angels weep,
Whispers of hope, secrets to keep.
Beneath the stars, prayers take flight,
Guided by faith, through darkest night.

In shadows deep, a heart ignites,
Seeking the truth, in gentle rites.
A sacred bond, the spirit's grace,
In every tear, we find our place.

Voices entwined, in hymns of peace,
The soul's longing shall never cease.
With every step, the path unfolds,
Stories of love, in whispers told.

Amidst the trials, we shall rise,
Turning our gaze toward the skies.
With reverence bowed, we walk this way,
Guided by light, come what may.

In shadows cast, we find the spark,
A flame of faith, ignites the dark.
For in each heart, a beacon shines,
Carving the way, as spirit aligns.

Chains of Devotion

Bound by the love that knows no end,
In humble hearts, true faith we send.
Chains of devotion, unbreakable ties,
Through trials faced, our spirit flies.

In every moment, grace bestowed,
In silent prayers, our burdens load.
Hands lifted high, in sacrifice,
We journey forth, through pain and ice.

Through storms we weather, side by side,
In unity's strength, we shall abide.
Each step a promise, each word a vow,
In chains of devotion, we take our bow.

With love as compass, we seek the truth,
A testament born from age of youth.
In every heartbeat, a song of peace,
Together we thrive, in love's release.

As souls entwined, our spirits glow,
In chains of devotion, we truly know.
For in this journey, all hearts align,
Forever bound, your hand in mine.

Graceful Encounters

In sacred moments, grace unfolds,
Each encounter, a story told.
With eyes that see, and hearts that hear,
In gentle whispers, love draws near.

In every soul, a light divine,
Connecting threads of love entwined.
With open arms, we greet the day,
In graceful encounters, we kneel and pray.

A smile shared, a hand in need,
Transforming lives with loving deeds.
In simple acts, the spirit flows,
Through graceful encounters, kindness grows.

With gratitude, we share this space,
In every challenge, we find grace.
Together we walk, hand in hand,
In the beauty of life, we understand.

So let us cherish, each fleeting chance,
In every meeting, a sacred dance.
With grateful hearts, we'll make our mark,
In graceful encounters, igniting spark.

Labors of Love

In every toil, a purpose found,
With hands that serve, on holy ground.
Laboring hard for the greater good,
In the name of love, we bravely stood.

Through trials faced, we lift each other,
In the warmth of trust, we find our mother.
For in our deeds, the truth we show,
Labors of love, through high and low.

With every heartbeat, we weave the thread,
In unity's strength, no fear or dread.
Together we rise, in laughter and tears,
Building the future, conquering fears.

For love's great labor, we're called to serve,
In every action, we find the nerve.
In the harvest shared, our joy we claim,
Through labors of love, we seek His name.

So let our work be a sacred song,
In harmony lived, where we belong.
With every effort, our spirits soar,
In labors of love, forevermore.

Flames of Reverence

In the quiet glow of night,
We gather 'round the sacred fire,
Hearts ablaze with pure delight,
Our spirits lifted, ever higher.

Songs of old rise from the soul,
Voices blend in harmony,
With each note, we feel whole,
In unity, we find our glee.

The warmth encircles every prayer,
Embers dance like whispered hopes,
As love ignites the hearts laid bare,
Through faith's light, our spirit copes.

In the flames, the truth reveals,
Ancient tales of love and grace,
Through trials, our devotion seals,
In this moment, we embrace.

As the fire begins to wane,
We carry forth this sacred light,
In reverence, we break the chain,
Guided by faith, through the night.

Anointed Heavy Hearts

Anointed in the dawn's soft dew,
Heavy hearts await the sun,
Through life's trials, we pursue,
Seeking solace as we run.

In shadows deep, where sorrows dwell,
We find strength in whispered prayers,
Each burden shared is less a hell,
In love's embrace, our spirit repairs.

With tears like rain, we wash our pain,
Giving voice to what we bear,
In sacred trust, will we remain,
Hand in hand, a bond we share.

So let the oil of grace anoint,
Our heavy hearts, a sweet release,
Through trials passed, our souls anoint,
In faith and love, we find our peace.

Together, we rise from the fall,
Hearts made light through holy ties,
In every echo, we hear the call,
In unity, our spirit flies.

Everlasting Cargo

Beneath the weight of fleeting days,
We carry forth our sacred cargo,
With each step, the spirit sways,
In faith, our hearts shall never slow.

Through storms and sun, we journey on,
With burdens shared, our load is light,
A constant song, like fragile dawn,
Where shadows yield to morning light.

In every trial, in every tear,
We gather strength from those before,
An everlasting love draws near,
Its gentle grace forevermore.

Our cargo holds the tales of yore,
Of courage found in darkest times,
In every heart, a guiding lore,
In unity, our spirit climbs.

So let us tread on paths anew,
With every step, our bond will grow,
In love and faith, we will break through,
An everlasting glow we sow.

Communion with Our Past

In the stillness, we find our way,
To echoes of those who came before,
Through whispered prayers, we long to stay,
In communion with our sacred lore.

Each memory a guiding light,
Illuminating paths once trod,
In reverence, we embrace the night,
Our hearts entwined with the hand of God.

Let the stories wrap us tight,
Like arms of love around our soul,
In faith, we seek enduring sight,
As history makes our spirits whole.

Through trials faced and battles won,
We gather strength from times gone by,
In every breath, their work not done,
In gratitude, we lift our cry.

Together, we forge ahead,
With wisdom gleaned from ages past,
In every prayer, their love is shed,
A blessing strong, forever cast.

Ascent with Obscured Eyes

In shadows cast by whispered doubt,
We seek the light beyond the veil.
Each step a prayer upon the route,
As faith prevails where truth may sail.

The summit calls with gentle grace,
Yet veils obscure the path we tread.
In silent faith we find our place,
And learn to see where others dread.

Through mist we climb, hearts intertwined,
Bound to the hope that guides our flight.
In weary souls, a strength we find,
With every step we claim the light.

So let the journey be our song,
With every note a humble plea.
In unity, we all belong,
For love shall set our spirits free.

With obscured eyes, we will not hide,
In trust we rise, our hearts ablaze.
Together, on this holy ride,
We walk the path that faith displays.

A Psalm of Portage

Through trials faced upon this shore,
We lift our voices to the sky.
Each burden borne, a sacred lore,
In every tear, a whispered sigh.

O mighty hands that guide our way,
Bestow your strength in darkest night.
For in our hearts, we long to stay,
Close by your side, a beacon bright.

The rivers flow, we sail with grace,
Through storms that roar and seas that churn.
Our souls find rest in your embrace,
As weary hearts through you discern.

With every turn, we heed the call,
To carry forth the love you breathe.
In unity, we rise and fall,
With trust in you, we learn to cleave.

A psalm of thanks for guidance shared,
For journeys bound in faith and light.
In every heart, your love declared,
With hope and grace, our souls take flight.

Chains and Chalices of the Soul

In solitude, we bear our chains,
Each link a story etched in scars.
Yet in the pain, a love remains,
A light that shines beyond the stars.

With every chalice raised in praise,
We find redemption in the fray.
Though heavy hearts may feel the blaze,
In shared embrace, we find our way.

For every burden has its grace,
In trials faced, our spirits grow.
In comfort found, we find our place,
Through every joy, through every woe.

Chains bind, yet also teach the soul,
To seek the strength that dwells within.
In every heart, we are made whole,
A cycle true where love begins.

So raise the chalice high and free,
To celebrate the path we forge.
In chains and chalices, we see,
The tapestry of life emerge.

The Sacrificial Path We Walk

In shadows deep, the path laid bare,
We tread the soil of sacred grace.
Each sacrifice, a whispered prayer,
A mirror held to love's embrace.

Through valleys low, with faith we roam,
For every tear, a blessing gained.
In surrender, we find our home,
With every heartache, joy reclaimed.

The road is steep, yet forward still,
With courage drawn from love's decree.
In yielding, find the deeper will,
The light that shines through agony.

With lifted hands, we walk the way,
To bear the weight of grief and grace.
In every step, our souls will sway,
Together, seek the holy place.

Thus keep your heart in perfect peace,
For in the trial, faith shall grow.
On this path, our spirits cease,
In sacrificial love, we glow.

The Weight of Unseen Graces

In silent prayers we rise and bow,
With hearts alight, we seek the vow.
In shadows cast, there lies His grace,
We tread on paths, though we may face.

Through trials met, our spirits soar,
Each burden lightens, love restores.
In kindness shared, a whisper flows,
The weight we bear, in peace it grows.

Though doubts may creep, we stand in light,
With faith bestowed, we share the fight.
A gentle hand, a shared embrace,
In unity, we find our place.

Among the thorns, the blooms arise,
Each moment held, a sweet surprise.
Divine intention, woven tight,
In every heart, ignites the light.

Thus in our trials, hope remains,
The song of grace in joyful strains.
We share the weight, though it is vast,
With unseen love, the die is cast.

Reverence in Our Labors

With hands that toil, our spirits rise,
In every task, His love's the prize.
We build with care, foundations strong,
In humble hearts, we find our song.

For every seed that we do sow,
In quiet fields, true blessings grow.
Our sweat and tears, a sacred stream,
In faith we work, we dare to dream.

With grateful hearts, we face the day,
In every challenge, come what may.
The labor sweet, the struggle real,
In reverence, His grace we feel.

In unity, our voices blend,
We carry forth, our hearts we send.
In sacred rhythm, life unfolds,
Each story told, the truth it holds.

Thus in our work, joy intertwines,
With purpose clear, in sacred signs.
In every breath, through toil and strife,
We build His kingdom, gift of life.

Sacred Stones We Bear

Each stone we carry, weight divine,
A testament of paths we find.
In every struggle, lessons learned,
Through trials met, our hearts have turned.

With every burden that we share,
In unity, we feel His care.
The sacred stones, a journey's guide,
In faith we walk, with Him beside.

Through rocky paths, our spirit grows,
In every heartbeat, love bestows.
The strength we find, a sacred grace,
In every trial, His warm embrace.

As mountains stand, so too our will,
In every vow, His promise still.
With sacred stones, we forge our way,
In every dawn, a brand new day.

Through sacred stones, our stories blend,
In unity, we love and mend.
With faith renewed, we rise and care,
Let love surround, our burdens share.

Echoes of Ancients on Shoulders

In whispers soft, the ancients call,
Their echoes strong within us all.
With wisdom deep, they guide our tread,
On shoulders broad, their truths are spread.

From distant shores, their tales resound,
In every heart, their love is found.
We carry forth their sacred lore,
In every step, we seek to soar.

Through trials faced, their strength we hold,
In sacred texts, their stories bold.
The world transforms, when love is near,
In echoes loud, their voices clear.

Each lesson shared, a bond we weave,
In every moment, grace we cleave.
With ancient wisdom lighting our way,
We walk in faith, come what may.

Thus, in our hearts, the ancients dwell,
With every breath, their truths we tell.
Together we rise, united and free,
In echoes of love, our legacy.

Devotion Woven in Weight

In shadows deep, my spirit cries,
With each tear, I find my prize.
The cloak of grief, yet pure and bright,
In whispers soft, I seek the light.

Through burdens borne, I rise anew,
In faith's embrace, my heart breaks through.
Each heavy thought a thread in loom,
In love's warm glow, dispels the gloom.

With aching hands, I weave my prayer,
A tapestry of hope laid bare.
Through trials faced, my soul ascends,
In every stitch, a heart that mends.

Oh sacred bond, my anchor line,
In tangled paths, Your grace I find.
Amidst the storms, Your voice I hear,
My steadfast guide, forever near.

Until the dawn breaks through the night,
In every sorrow, finds the light.
Devotion strong, through trials faced,
In love's embrace, I'll find my place.

The Silent Joins of Faith

In quiet moments, faith does swell,
With tender grace, the heart will tell.
Each silent sigh, a prayer's release,
In tranquil stillness, shadows cease.

With every heartbeat, I confess,
In solitude, I find my rest.
The softest echo in the night,
In shadows cast, I seek the light.

The silent joins, like threads in loom,
Weaving strength within the gloom.
In whispered hope, my spirit lifts,
Each gentle touch, a presence gifts.

Through quiet paths and whispered songs,
With humble hearts, where faith belongs.
The silent dance, where souls align,
In still communion, divine design.

Beneath the stars, my heart will soar,
In silent trust, forevermore.
For in the stillness, truth reveals,
A love that guides, a heart that heals.

Illuminated by Woe

In tears that flow, the heart takes flight,
Illumined by sorrow, shadows fight.
With every ache, a truth unveiled,
In darkest night, my spirit sailed.

Through shattered dreams, I find my way,
In brokenness, my hopes convey.
The path of grief, a winding road,
Where every burden shares its load.

In whispered grace, I find my peace,
From every wound, a love's release.
Illuminated by bitter tears,
In every sigh, compassion nears.

Each hurting soul a candle bright,
In woe's embrace, we find the light.
Through trials faced, we stand as one,
In unity, our hearts are spun.

In darkened valleys, hope does gleam,
For through our pain, we dare to dream.
Illuminated by love's embrace,
In every heart, we find our place.

The Pilgrimage of Heavy Thoughts

On winding roads where shadows lay,
I tread the path, both night and day.
Each heavy thought, a weight I bear,
In pilgrimage, I find Your care.

With every step, my spirit seeks,
In whispered prayers, my silence speaks.
The burdens shared, like waves of sea,
In faith's embrace, I long to be.

Through mountains high and valleys low,
Each heavy thought begins to flow.
In toil and trial, I find my strand,
A journey forged, a guiding hand.

With steadfast heart, I wander still,
Through every tempest, You fulfill.
The pilgrimage, a sacred quest,
In every tear, my soul's caressed.

For in the weight, I find my grace,
In every moment, Your embrace.
The heavy thoughts, like clouds of rain,
In love's soft light, they shift to gain.

Heavenly Luggage

We carry our burdens, light as a breeze,
With faith as our anchor, we sail with ease.
In the depths of our hearts, love's treasure we store,
Each moment a blessing, forever and more.

The heavens above, they whisper to us,
In times of distress, we find our trust.
Our souls intertwined, like vines we ascend,
With heavenly luggage, our spirits extend.

The road may be rocky, the path often steep,
Yet we gather our hopes, and God's promises keep.
In the laughter of angels, we find our way,
Heavenly luggage, guiding each day.

Through trials we travel, our faith as a guide,
In the solace of prayer, we find peace inside.
With every step taken beneath the vast sky,
We lift our hearts higher, to the heavens we fly.

Our burdens transformed into wings of light,
With every single prayer, we embrace the night.
The weight of the world, like dust, it will fall,
For in the grace of God, we find strength for all.

Faithful Encumbrances

In the journey of life, we bear faithful loads,
Each purpose we carry, a message unfolds.
Though heavy the weight may sometimes appear,
We trust in His promise, for He is our spear.

Our burdens reflect what we hold in our hearts,
They teach us of love, compassion imparts.
Through trials and tribulations, our spirits unite,
Faithful encumbrances shine through the night.

The path may be winding, the tempests may roar,
Yet hand in hand, we'll traverse every shore.
With the grace of the Savior lighting our way,
Faithful encumbrances guide us each day.

Each sorrow that comes, like rain on the fields,
Will nourish our souls, as love gently yields.
In the circle of life, we dance and we pray,
Faithful encumbrances lead us toward day.

So let not our burdens weigh down our soul,
They mold us with wisdom, make us more whole.
In the tapestry woven, our stories align,
With faithful encumbrances, His love will shine.

Spiritual Waters

Beneath the vast skies, the waters flow free,
A wellspring of grace, quenching our plea.
In currents of love, we are gently swept,
With spiritual waters, our hearts are kept.

The ripples of kindness expand as they glide,
Embracing all souls, with arms open wide.
In the depths of the river, wisdom will dwell,
Spiritual waters, a comforting well.

When storms rage above, and shadows loom near,
We dip into faith, find solace sincere.
Cleansed by His mercy, we rise and restore,
Spiritual waters forever will pour.

Each droplet a story, of trials and peace,
In the ocean of love, our burdens release.
As we flow with the tide, let our spirits soar,
Spiritual waters, forever we adore.

So gather your fears, let them sink out of view,
Trust in the promise, His love will renew.
In the embrace of the waves, we find our home,
Spiritual waters, where we freely roam.

Cloaks of Memory

In the fabric of time, our stories are sewn,
Cloaks of memory gather, cherished and known.
Each thread woven tight, with love and with care,
Holding moments of grace, captured in prayer.

The laughter of friends wrapped in warmth of our soul,
In the kindness of strangers, we learn to be whole.
Through journeys and trials, the lessons we glean,
Cloaks of memory, a tapestry seen.

In shadows we wander, in light we find cheer,
Reminders of faith echo crystal and clear.
Though seasons may fade, and paths may depart,
Cloaks of memory shelter the warmth of the heart.

Each fabric a piece of the life that we share,
Holding whispers of hope, like a soft gentle prayer.
Through the winds of the past, where time softly bends,
Cloaks of memory bind us, as love never ends.

As we gather these moments, like jewels in the night,
We wear them with pride, in His radiant light.
In the tapestry woven, may we always see,
Cloaks of memory, made divine by decree.

Prayer of the Worn and Weary

O Lord, hear my humble plea,
In shadows deep, I long for Thee.
My heart is heavy, burdened soul,
Guide me, Lord, to making whole.

In trials faced and battles lost,
I seek Your strength, no matter the cost.
With weary hands, I call your name,
In faith renewed, I'll fan the flame.

Each step I take, a prayer I weave,
In strife and doubt, I still believe.
Lift me up, O hand divine,
In Your embrace, I seek to shine.

Though storms may rage, I stand my ground,
In silence, Your holy voice is found.
In darkest nights, You are my light,
A beacon pure, my heart's delight.

So grant me peace, O gentle guide,
In Your love, I will abide.
With every breath, I praise Your name,
Forever blessed, I'll never be the same.

A Faithful Load

Upon this path, I tread alone,
With burdens grasped and seeds I've sown.
Each step a testament of grace,
In every trial, I find Your face.

O faithful Lord, my guiding star,
In every struggle, near or far.
Though heavy hangs the load I bear,
You lift me high with loving care.

Rivers of sorrow may flow today,
Yet in Your truth, I choose to stay.
Your strength, my anchor in the storm,
Through faithfulness, my spirit's warm.

In burdens shared and joys revealed,
The faithful heart shall never yield.
With each dawn's light, I rise anew,
In every challenge, I trust in You.

A faithful load, I bear in love,
With eyes set firm on skies above.
I know Your presence guides my way,
In every heartache, come what may.

Tabernacle of Troubling Times

In this tabernacle, shadows creep,
But faith within my heart shall leap.
Troubling times may cloud my view,
Yet Your spirit breathes me through.

A shelter strong in storms we seek,
In whispered prayers, I find the weak.
O shield of grace, my refuge near,
In every struggle, You are here.

Through trials fierce, I hear Your call,
In every rise, I shall not fall.
Your light, a beacon in my night,
With every step, You guide my flight.

The burdens lift, my heart repaired,
In sweet surrender, I am bared.
With open arms, I seek Your grace,
In troubling times, I find my place.

In faith, I gather strength anew,
With every heartbeat, I adore You.
This tabernacle, where I reside,
In dark and light, You are my guide.

Offering Up Our Burdens

With open hands, I seek to give,
Each burdened weight that I outlive.
O Lord, I lay my cares at Your feet,
In humble trust, I find retreat.

Offering up the fears I hold,
In Your warm presence, I am consoled.
Each tear a token, every sigh,
Reshaped by grace, my soul to fly.

The chains of worry start to break,
In loving arms, I find my strength.
With faith restored, I walk this road,
As You, O Lord, my heart have strode.

In trials deep and paths unknown,
I hand my burdens, make them Your own.
Your gentle whisper calms my mind,
Within Your love, true peace I find.

So take my heart, my fears, my all,
In Your embrace, I'll never fall.
Offering up my weary strife,
In sacred love, I find my life.

Worn Boots of Belief

With worn boots I wander forth,
Through fields of sorrow, light and mirth.
Each step a prayer, each breath a hymn,
In faith's embrace, my heart won't dim.

The path is rugged, steep and wide,
Yet in His love, I will abide.
The stones beneath, they guide my way,
In whispers soft, He'll never stray.

Each puddle mirrors His gentle grace,
Reflections of love in every place.
With every mile, my spirit grows,
Rooted deep, His truth now glows.

Through trials faced, and shadows cast,
The journey holds the love amassed.
With every sunrise, a chance to see,
In worn boots, I walk with Thee.

So let my boots bear witness true,
To all the wonders I pursue.
In faith so strong, I now believe,
With worn boots of truth, I shall receive.

Traces of the Divine

In morning light, the world awakes,
With gentle whispers, grace it makes.
A soft breeze carries tales untold,
Of sacred love that won't grow old.

The rustle of leaves, a sacred sound,
In nature's choir, His voice is found.
Every petal, a testament,
Of beauty where His love is sent.

Stars above shimmer like dreams,
In cosmic dance, divine it seems.
With every glimmer, a chance to seek,
The quiet voice that makes us speak.

In laughter shared and tears that flow,
Traces of Him in hearts do grow.
With every bond, a hand divine,
In every moment, His love we find.

So let us cherish all we see,
The sacred notes in every spree.
For in our lives, He leaves His mark,
In traces of love, a holy spark.

Heartstrings and Haversacks

With heartstrings pulled in love's embrace,
We wander life, a sacred space.
In haversacks, our dreams we fold,
Carrying stories yet untold.

Each moment shines as a precious gift,
In laughter's light, our spirits lift.
Through trials met, through joy's delight,
We find His path, our guiding light.

With every burden, we learn to lean,
On faith and hope, the unseen seam.
In every heartache, wisdom grows,
In love's warm glow, our courage shows.

The road ahead may twist and turn,
But in His arms, our souls we yearn.
With every step, our faith we weave,
In heartstrings strong, we shall believe.

So let our haversacks be light,
Filled with love, our spirits bright.
With heartstrings bound, we walk as one,
In every dusk, a rising sun.

Altars in Our Hearts

Within the quiet, altars rise,
In hearts adorned, pure love complies.
Candles flicker with hope anew,
In sacred space, we find what's true.

Each prayer lifted, a gentle sigh,
In moments hushed, we reach the sky.
With faithful hands and open minds,
We gather love that never blinds.

The weight of sorrow, we tenderly share,
As we build altars, laid with care.
In every tear, a drop of grace,
In every smile, we find His face.

Together we stand, through storm and sun,
With hearts united, we become one.
In every struggle, let us impart,
The strength we find in each other's heart.

So let us gather, the faithful few,
In altars of love, forever true.
For in our hearts, a light divine,
An altar built, where love will shine.

Embracing the Load of Love

In silence, we gather, hearts intertwined,
Beneath the weight of love, we are defined.
With every burden, our spirits align,
Together we rise, like the sun that will shine.

Through trials we wander, hand in hand,
In faith we surrender, together we stand.
Each tear a tribute, each sigh a prayer,
In love's embrace, we conquer despair.

We carry our stories, wrapped in His grace,
In hearts bound by mercy, we find our place.
The load is heavy, yet sweet is this plight,
In the depth of darkness, we seek the light.

With every heartbeat, we journey as one,
In the fabric of faith, our souls become spun.
Embracing the load, we shall never break,
For in each other's love, we awaken awake.

And when the night falls, we'll look to the stars,
Finding strength in our love, no matter the scars.
With voices united, we'll sing through the pain,
Embracing the load, the love we have gained.

Sacred Trials and Ephemeral Ties

In the face of struggle, we find our truth,
With sacred trials, we nourish our youth.
Each moment a lesson, each failure a guide,
In ephemeral ties, our souls collide.

Through shadows we wander, seeking the grace,
In the depths of turmoil, we find our place.
With whispers of faith, our spirits unite,
Together we stand in the long, lonely night.

For every storm that shadows our way,
In divine connection, we choose to stay.
Through echoes of pain, we rise from the fall,
In sacred trials, we answer the call.

The fleeting connections, like dew on the rose,
A reminder of love that eternally flows.
With hands lifted high, we seek to ascend,
In sacred trials, our hearts will not bend.

In laughter and sorrow, we journey as one,
With faith in our hearts, the battle is won.
With each sacred trial, a purpose we find,
For love is eternal, a bond that's divine.

Comfort in Our Collective Struggles

In the arms of each other, we gather as kin,
Finding comfort in struggles, where healing begins.
With shared aspirations, we lighten the load,
In the warmth of compassion, our spirits explode.

Through trials unspoken and burdens we bear,
In whispers of hope, we learn to repair.
With every hardship, a lesson we find,
In the depth of our hearts, compassion is kind.

Through the storms of our lives, we weather the night,
Together we shine, like stars in their flight.
In unity's embrace, we conquer the fears,
With comfort in struggle, we wipe away tears.

For in every echo of love that we share,
We cultivate strength, a bond we declare.
Through laughter and sorrow, we hold each other tight,
In the comfort of faith, we emerge into light.

In the garden of hope, our spirits will grow,
Through collective struggles, together we flow.
With love as our anchor, we rise and ascend,
Finding comfort in struggles, where hearts learn to mend.

The Anvil of Divine Endurance

In the fires of struggle, we melt and renew,
On the anvil of faith, our strength we pursue.
With each strike of hardship, our souls are refined,
In the heart of endurance, true power we find.

The lessons are heavy, the burdens are vast,
Yet with every trial, we're forged from the past.
In patience we wait, through darkness we dream,
On the anvil of love, we flow like a stream.

For every temptation that knocks at the door,
We stand in His light, we will not ignore.
With courage as armor, we face what may come,
On the anvil of grace, we know we are home.

Through fires of hardship, our spirits take flight,
In the rhythm of struggle, we find our true might.
With hearts that are open, we let go of fear,
On the anvil of life, our purpose is clear.

In unity's forge, together we're strong,
With faith as our melody, we rise in song.
Through the trials we bear, our legacy blooms,
On the anvil of divine, our love brightly looms.

Wounds and Wonders

In shadows whisper grace divine,
The broken heart, a sacred sign.
From ashes sprout the blooms of hope,
In pain, we learn to rise and cope.

Through trials forged, our spirit grows,
Each wound a path the seeker knows.
With hands outstretched to touch the light,
Wonders bloom within the night.

Beneath the weight of heavy chains,
A melody in sorrow reigns.
With every tear, a prayer we weave,
In loss, we find what we believe.

Yet in the depths, a spark remains,
Faith ignites, and love sustains.
So let us walk on sacred ground,
In wounds, the wonders shall be found.

Together bound in silent grace,
We find our hope in every place.
For through our wounds, we shall transcend,
In wondrous love, our souls shall mend.

Burdened Blessings

In heavy hearts, the blessings dwell,
Each burden lifted, tells a tale.
With whispered prayers, we rise anew,
Finding strength in all we do.

Through darkest nights, the stars align,
Each trial faced, a holy sign.
The weight we bear, a sacred trust,
In faith, we rise from earthly dust.

Our hands may tremble, spirits ache,
Yet in the silence, we awake.
With every tear, a seed is sown,
Through pain, our faith is brightly grown.

In every challenge, blessings grace,
The scars we bear, a warm embrace.
Together, side by side we stand,
In burdens born, we understand.

The journey's long, the path is steep,
Yet in our hearts, the promise deep.
With gratitude, we walk the road,
In every burden, blessings flowed.

Litanies of Silent Struggles

In quiet tomorrows, we reflect,
The struggles faced, the wounds we check.
Through litanies of whispered pain,
A chorus sings, we rise again.

With every heartbeat, shadows creep,
Yet still we find the strength to leap.
In silent cries, a prayer ignites,
Transforming darkness into lights.

The battles fought behind closed doors,
Are sacred rites, our spirits soar.
Each struggle bears a lesson learned,
In all our trials, our souls are turned.

Together held in threads of grace,
We find our peace in learning's pace.
With every sigh, a hope restored,
In silent struggles, we're adored.

In unity, we stand in prayer,
With gentle hearts, we show we care.
Through litanies sung soft and low,
In silent strength, our spirits grow.

Pilgrimage of Heavy Hearts

On sacred trails, our journey starts,
With heavy loads and aching hearts.
Each step a prayer upon the ground,
In pilgrimage, our souls are found.

Through valleys deep and mountains tall,
In unity, we hear the call.
With every stumble, we arise,
Collecting blessings from the skies.

As sunlight breaks, our shadows fade,
In every heartache, love is laid.
With burdens shared, our laughter rings,
In heavy hearts, our spirit sings.

We walk the path that faith has drawn,
A pilgrimage from dusk till dawn.
With every tear, a grace unfolds,
In heavy hearts, our story's told.

So let us journey, hand in hand,
In every step, we understand.
Through faith and love, we'll find our part,
In pilgrimage, we heal the heart.

Shadows of the Soul

In quiet corners, shadows creep,
Whispers of sorrow, secrets deep.
Glimmers of hope, a guiding hand,
Hearts entwined in faith, they stand.

Beneath the weight of night's embrace,
Each soul seeks light, a sacred place.
In every tear, a river flows,
From darkest depths, the spirit grows.

Echoes of ancestors in our songs,
Their prayers shield us from the wrongs.
Together we rise, together we fall,
United in love, answering the call.

Through trials faced and time we spend,
In shadows' grasp, we find a friend.
The soul's rebirth, a gentle touch,
Guided by grace, we need so much.

In twilight's glow, shadows recede,
Hope's soft light, a vital seed.
From shadows' grasp, we shall not stray,
In faith's embrace, it lights the way.

Chains of Light

Bound by love, we wear our chains,
Each link a lesson, joy or pains.
With every trial, we grow more bright,
In darkness, we forge our chains of light.

From dawn's first kiss to twilight's sigh,
With every breath, our spirits fly.
These chains, though heavy, bear the grace,
Of every soul in this sacred space.

Connected hearts, we stand as one,
In strength and hope, the battle's won.
Each bond a promise, forever tight,
Unbroken, we shine, our chains of light.

Together we journey, hand in hand,
Through valleys deep and golden sand.
In every struggle, our spirits ignite,
Transforming burdens to chains of light.

So let us cherish these bonds we share,
For in our hearts, we find the care.
With every trial, we rise in might,
Embracing the love in chains of light.

Prayers on Our Shoulders

Beneath the weight of whispered prayers,
We walk the path, through joys and cares.
With every heartbeat, hope ascends,
A tapestry woven, love transcends.

In silent moments, we find our grace,
As burdens lift, we seek His face.
Together we carry each heavy load,
On shoulders strong, in love bestowed.

With faith as our shield, we face the storm,
In unity's strength, we are reborn.
Each prayer a beacon, guiding the way,
Through darkest nights, into the day.

In anguish met with sacred song,
We rise, we walk, where we belong.
Despite the trials, our spirits soar,
With prayers on shoulders, we yearn for more.

Together we stand, both bold and meek,
In love's embrace, it is Him we seek.
Prayers upon us, a blessed mold,
In every heart, His grace unfolds.

Divinity's Load

Upon our backs, divinity's load,
Each step we take, a sacred road.
With every burden, a chance to grow,
In trials faced, His light will show.

In quiet moments, we find the truth,
The strength of ages, the dreams of youth.
With faith as our banner, we shall strive,
In every heartbeat, the will to survive.

Through storms we weather, with heads held high,
Guided by stars that fill the sky.
Each challenge met, a purpose clear,
In divinity's load, we have no fear.

For in our struggles, we meet the divine,
A dance of shadows, a promise to shine.
With each heavy step, we march as one,
In love's embrace, the battle undone.

So let us carry this load with grace,
In faith's journey, we find our place.
Though heavy the load, we will not bend,
For divinity's strength will guide us till the end.

Strands of Devotion

In twilight's grace, we seek the light,
With whispers soft, our hearts take flight.
Each prayer a thread, a sacred weave,
In faith we stand, and we believe.

Beneath the stars, our souls ignite,
A tapestry of love shines bright.
In every breath, a promise made,
In every hope, our fears allayed.

Through trials steep, our spirits climb,
In unity, we transcend time.
With lifted hands, we find our way,
In trusting hearts, we choose to stay.

The river flows, our blessings stream,
In every tear, a holy dream.
Together bound, we share the grace,
In sacred spaces, we find our place.

With gentle hands, we plant the seeds,
Of love and care, for hearts in need.
In fervent prayer, we glimpse the dawn,
With strands of hope, our fears are gone.

Holy Imprints

In ancient texts, the wisdom glows,
A guiding light, where love bestows.
Each verse a mark on hearts so deep,
In echoes sweet, our souls do weep.

The sacred steps of those before,
In hallowed halls, their spirits soar.
Their holy imprints touch our lives,
In every breath, their spirit thrives.

With open eyes, we seek the truth,
In every child, in every youth.
The lessons learned, like stars aligned,
In every heart, a love refined.

In sacred songs, we share the fight,
With every note, we find the light.
A harmony of faith and grace,
In varied tongues, we find our place.

So let us walk this path of peace,
In every step, our doubts release.
For in the light, we have a friend,
A love that holds us, never bends.

Ancestral Echoes

In quiet woods, the echoes call,
Of ancestral love, who gave their all.
Their stories weave through sacred time,
In whispered tales, our spirits climb.

With every breath, their strength we feel,
In silent nights, their wounds will heal.
Through trials faced, their spirits guide,
In every heart, they now abide.

The roots run deep, entwined with faith,
In every tear, their gentle wraith.
Ancestral echoes whisper low,
In every heart, their love will grow.

A sacred bond, a timeless thread,
In every prayer, their hopes are fed.
Together bound, through loss and gain,
In every joy, their love remains.

So let us honor those who came,
With hearts aflame, we speak their name.
For in their footsteps, we shall find,
A love eternal, intertwined.

Weight of Salvation

In darkest nights, we seek the morn,
With heavy hearts, in love reborn.
Each burden shared, a sacred cost,
In every hope, we find what's lost.

Through trials fierce, we learn to stand,
With open hearts, we reach for hands.
The weight of sin, a heavy toll,
In whispered prayers, we make us whole.

The light descended, a holy grace,
In every heart, a sacred place.
Through sacrifice, our spirits soar,
In love's embrace, we seek no more.

With faith renewed, we rise again,
In every soul, the courage spin.
Through trials faced, we find release,
In gentle waves, we find our peace.

So let us carry this weight with pride,
In every heart, He walks beside.
For in our struggles, love shall reign,
In perfect grace, we break the chain.

Sanctified Sorrows and Shadows

In the valley of shadows we weep,
Yet hope in silence begins to seep.
Every tear a prayer, every sigh,
A whispered faith beneath the sky.

Fading lights illuminate the path,
Guiding hearts away from wrath.
In the depths, His love we find,
Sanctified sorrows, intertwined.

For in our breaking, He does mend,
Each heartache a chance to transcend.
With faith as armor, we push through,
Trusting grace in all we do.

Beneath the weight of heavy woes,
Lies the strength that only grows.
In sacred depths of suffering's night,
Emerges ever-hopeful light.

So let us carry our burdens high,
With lifted hearts, we will abide.
For every sorrow brings us near,
To the love that casts out fear.

Beneath the Armor of Suffering

Beneath the armor, pain does dwell,
In trials faced, we learn to tell.
Each scar a story, each wound a song,
In suffering's embrace, we belong.

With faith as our shield, we move ahead,
Trusting the path where angels tread.
Through the fire, our spirits rise,
In deepest valleys, we seek the skies.

The weight of sorrow teaches grace,
In the darkest times, we find our place.
With every trial, our hearts ignite,
A beacon of hope, a guiding light.

As thorns adorn the rose in bloom,
So too, our suffering brings forth room.
For wisdom gained and strength revealed,
In the heart of struggle, truth is sealed.

So let us walk this rugged road,
With love and faith, our heavy load.
For beneath the pain, we rise anew,
In sacred trust, our spirits grew.

The Altar of Our Trials

Upon the altar of our trials, we kneel,
With trembling hearts, our wounds to heal.
Each struggle faced, a sacred rite,
In darkness turned, we seek the light.

Through every tempest, faith will soar,
Resilient spirits seeking more.
In the crucible of pain, we stand,
United together, hand in hand.

For in our trials, His grace unfolds,
A tapestry of love, woven bold.
With every burden, we learn to pray,
Trusting His mercy lights the way.

In sacred whispers, His voice we find,
Unraveling fears that once confined.
Each hurdle crossed, redemption's call,
In unity of spirit, we give our all.

So let us honor every scar,
A testament of how far we are.
On the altar of our trials, we rise,
Transformed by grace beneath the skies.

Wounds as Testaments of Trust

Wounds are not signs of brokenness,
But testaments of faithfulness.
In every pain, a lesson learned,
In every trial, hope returned.

They tell the tale of battles fought,
Of silent prayers and lessons taught.
Through fire and storm, our spirits grow,
In the strength we find, His love will flow.

For trust is forged in darkest nights,
In shattered dreams, we find our sights.
Each scar a mark of victories won,
In the tapestry of life, we weave as one.

So let our wounds speak loud and clear,
In humble hearts, there is no fear.
For through our pain, His grace abounds,
In whispered love, the truth resounds.

Wounds as testaments, we carry forth,
A journey of faith, revealing worth.
With each step taken on this path,
We walk in trust, escaping wrath.

The Divine Embrace of Our Burden

In shadows deep, we kneel and pray,
Our heavy hearts, in silence stay.
Yet in the grasp of holy light,
We find our strength to face the night.

Each burden bore, a gift to share,
In trials faced, we learn to care.
Through pain and loss, a path unfolds,
Where love's warm grace forever holds.

With every tear, a seed is sown,
The trials transform us, flesh and bone.
In sacred trust, we lift our gaze,
To feel the warmth of heaven's blaze.

The weight we carry draws us near,
In faith, we find our vision clear.
Together bound by sacred thread,
We walk the path where angels tread.

So let the burdens guide our way,
To holy realms where spirits play.
In every step, His love imparts,
The bond of grace in weary hearts.

Chronicles of the Weighed Down

In lands of sorrow, we find the tale,
Of weary souls whose hopes prevail.
With every trial, a truth descends,
That love will guide our broken bends.

The stones we carry, heavy still,
Become the forge to shape our will.
In every wound, a lesson waits,
To turn our grief to open gates.

We gather close, in silent prayer,
As burdens shared becomes a flair.
Through whispered faith and gentle hands,
We rise above in holy bands.

Each chronicle, a sacred light,
Illuminating darkest night.
With every shadow cast away,
We stand united, come what may.

For in the weight, we find our song,
A melody where we belong.
In unity, we claim our cries,
And lift our voices to the skies.

Conduits of Carrying Faith

In valleys low, we sow our seeds,
As conduits of hope, fulfilling needs.
With every step, our spirits rise,
A testament beneath the skies.

Through trials faced, our faith ignites,
In darkest hours, we seek the lights.
With open arms, we bear the weight,
As love's embrace transcends our fate.

In every burden, a chance to grow,
As rivers of faith begin to flow.
Together strong, we lift the veil,
With open hearts, we will not fail.

Conduits blessed from above to below,
In acts of kindness, our spirits glow.
The ties we forge, a sacred bond,
In unity, of love we're fond.

So let our faith be that which unites,
A beacon shining through the nights.
In courage bold, let us proclaim,
Our burdens shared, in love's sweet name.

Tides of Grace in Our Labor

Upon the shores of toil and tears,
We labor on despite our fears.
For in each wave, a grace we find,
To soothe the weary, heal the blind.

As tides arise and challenges flow,
We dig in deep, our roots will grow.
Through sweat and strife, we bear the weight,
In every struggle, love creates.

With open hearts, our hands are free,
To lift each soul to destiny.
Through every task, we find the grace,
In labor's song, a warm embrace.

Together bound by duty's call,
In faith we stand, we shall not fall.
For with each tide that sweeps the shore,
We learn that love will ever soar.

So let the waves of grace abound,
In every heart, His love resounds.
In labor's cry, we find our peace,
As tides of grace bring sweet release.

Burdens of Faith

In shadows deep, our spirits cry,
With every step, we learn to fly.
Through trials fierce, our hearts will swell,
In burdens borne, we find hope's well.

In whispered prayers, our worries fade,
The light within shall never shade.
Each weight we bear, a chance to grow,
In faith's embrace, our souls aglow.

Through deserts vast, we seek the stream,
In praise and trust, we weave our dream.
In darkness clings the steadfast light,
Our burdens shared in love's pure sight.

Each moment spent in silent plea,
Unleashes strength, sets spirits free.
For when we falter, grace shall rise,
With every dawn, our spirits try.

So let us march through life's great test,
With courage strong, we find our rest.
In burdens borne, a future bright,
In faith we walk, our guiding light.

Celestial Troves

In heavens high, a treasure glows,
Beyond the stars, where pure love flows.
In radiant beams, our spirits soar,
To seek the troves, forevermore.

Each prayer a key, each wish a door,
To hidden realms, where spirits soar.
In stillness found, the truth remains,
Through whispered hopes, divine refrains.

The paths of light, they gently guide,
In sacred truths, we learn to bide.
In every heart, a flame so bright,
A source of warmth in darkest night.

O seeker, trust the journey's way,
Through trials faced, we learn to pray.
For in the depths of every soul,
Lies a celestial trove, our goal.

So lift your gaze, and feel the grace,
In every moment, find your place.
In celestial troves, we find our claim,
United in love, in spirit's name.

Burdens of Faith

In shadows deep, our spirits cry,
With every step, we learn to fly.
Through trials fierce, our hearts will swell,
In burdens borne, we find hope's well.

In whispered prayers, our worries fade,
The light within shall never shade.
Each weight we bear, a chance to grow,
In faith's embrace, our souls aglow.

Through deserts vast, we seek the stream,
In praise and trust, we weave our dream.
In darkness clings the steadfast light,
Our burdens shared in love's pure sight.

Each moment spent in silent plea,
Unleashes strength, sets spirits free.
For when we falter, grace shall rise,
With every dawn, our spirits try.

So let us march through life's great test,
With courage strong, we find our rest.
In burdens borne, a future bright,
In faith we walk, our guiding light.

Celestial Troves

In heavens high, a treasure glows,
Beyond the stars, where pure love flows.
In radiant beams, our spirits soar,
To seek the troves, forevermore.

Each prayer a key, each wish a door,
To hidden realms, where spirits soar.
In stillness found, the truth remains,
Through whispered hopes, divine refrains.

The paths of light, they gently guide,
In sacred truths, we learn to bide.
In every heart, a flame so bright,
A source of warmth in darkest night.

O seeker, trust the journey's way,
Through trials faced, we learn to pray.
For in the depths of every soul,
Lies a celestial trove, our goal.

So lift your gaze, and feel the grace,
In every moment, find your place.
In celestial troves, we find our claim,
United in love, in spirit's name.

Lessons from the Path

Upon this path, the lessons grow,
In every step, the seeds we sow.
Through winding ways, our wisdom lies,
In every tear, a new sunrise.

The stones we stumble, the roots that bind,
They shape our hearts, they test our mind.
In every breath, a chance to learn,
With each embrace, the hearts will burn.

For in the trials, we find our strength,
In faith's embrace, we go the length.
Each heartbeat echoes the lessons heard,
In silence shared, the spoken word.

The journey's tale, in shadows cast,
Reminds us all, its lessons vast.
Through joy and pain, we come to see,
The path unfolds our destiny.

So take each step with open soul,
For every lesson makes us whole.
In lessons learned, we find our peace,
From paths once walked, our fears will cease.

Vestiges of Longing

In every heart, longings dwell,
Whispers soft as twilight's bell.
Through valleys deep, our wishes cry,
In search of truth, we reach the sky.

The stars above, they blink and gleam,
In shadows cast, we chase the dream.
With every prayer, a hope unfolds,
In vestiges of love, the heart beholds.

For every tear that stains the night,
Reflects our quest for purest light.
In yearning deep, our spirits yearn,
Through love's embrace, our souls will burn.

In silence held, we seek the grace,
To find our longings' sacred space.
Through trials faced and paths we roam,
In vestiges of longing, we find home.

So cherish each dream, let it unfurl,
In every beat, the universe swirls.
For in longing's depths, we find the key,
To all we are and all we'll be.

Silent Burdens

In shadows deep, our hearts do speak,
With whispered prayers, our souls they seek.
The weight we bear, so oft unseen,
Yet in His love, our hope is keen.

Through trials fierce, we find our way,
A guiding light that will not sway.
In silent burdens, grace is found,
As mercy's song does all surround.

In quiet moments, faith takes flight,
Transforming darkness into light.
We rise anew, with spirits bold,
In holy warmth, our fears consoled.

With heavy hearts, we learn to stand,
Embracing peace, we join His band.
Each tear a prayer, each sigh a song,
In unity, we all belong.

So as we walk, let love lead on,
For silent burdens will be gone.
In faith we trust, and in His grace,
We find our home, a sacred space.

Sacred Weights

Upon our shoulders, burdens laid,
In sacred trust, we are conveyed.
With every step, our spirits rise,
Towards the heavens, our voices sigh.

The weight of love, so pure and true,
In trials faced, we are made new.
Through every storm, we learn to bend,
For in His hands, our hearts transcend.

Each moment's pause, a chance to pray,
To lift the weights we bear each day.
In fellowship, we find our strength,
As sacred weights unite at length.

With every breath, we seek His grace,
The trials faced become a trace.
Of faith renewed and visions clear,
In sacred weights, we draw Him near.

Through valleys low and mountains high,
We walk in faith, we do not shy.
For when we share these burdens laced,
We find the joy of love embraced.

Echoes of the Heart

In echoes soft, the Spirit speaks,
A whispered truth that gently seeks.
Each heart a vessel, pure and bright,
Reflecting love, our guiding light.

With every beat, a prayer resounds,
In sacred silence, grace abounds.
The heart's desire, a flame held strong,
In echoes deep, we find our song.

Through trials faced, and paths unsure,
The echoes call us to endure.
In deepest sorrow, hope is sown,
With every echo, love is grown.

A gentle nudge, a soft embrace,
In echoes, we discover grace.
Each heartbeat pulses with His will,
In echoes of the heart, we still.

Together bound, in faith we rise,
With open hearts beneath the skies.
In every echo, life imparts,
The timeless truth of sacred hearts.

Gifts of the Wanderer

In journeys vast, we roam the lands,
Collecting gifts in open hands.
With every step, we find our way,
The wanderer's heart is meant to stray.

Through mountains high and valleys deep,
In whispered winds, His secrets keep.
Each lesson learned, a treasure gained,
In gifts of grace, our souls are trained.

The wanderer's path is never clear,
But faith directs, and love draws near.
With every step, we learn to see,
The beauty in His mystery.

In fleeting moments, joy unfolds,
A story shared, a heart that holds.
For in our wanderings, we find,
The gifts bestowed, forever kind.

So let us walk with heads held high,
In every gift, a sacred sigh.
For wanderers share a common song,
In love we find where we belong.

Conversations with the Stars

In the silent night we gaze and ponder,
Heavens whisper secrets, wonders yonder.
Each twinkle tells a tale of ages,
Mirrored in our hearts like sacred pages.

Oh, let us speak with the distant lights,
Drawn to their glow on celestial nights.
Guiding our thoughts, they sparkle so bright,
Reminding us of love, shining in sight.

In dreams we wander, embrace the divine,
Stars become our homes, forever they shine.
Universal truths in their glow we find,
In sparkling silence, our souls entwined.

We listen closely, hearts open wide,
Each star a message, our faithful guide.
In that vastness lies a promise so near,
Conversations with stars, whispering clear.

So as we reach for the cosmic embrace,
With every heartbeat, we touch endless space.
In the tapestry of night, we unite,
Conversations with stars, our spirits take flight.

Mosaic of Memories

Life's moments weave a tapestry bright,
Each thread a story, bathed in soft light.
Shimmering fragments of laughter and tears,
A mosaic of memories, echoing years.

From whispered hopes to dreams that reside,
In the chambers of heart, where love does abide.
Faded photographs and voices we hear,
Connect us to those we cherish most dear.

Time flows like rivers, winding and wise,
Carving through valleys, beneath vast skies.
Every step taken, a beat in the dance,
Moments entwined in a sacred romance.

A smile, a tear, they blend ever near,
Crafting our stories, bringing us cheer.
In the gallery of life, we find our way,
A mosaic of memories brightens the day.

So cherish each fragment, let them inspire,
In the sacred collection, we never tire.
For every memory is a piece of the art,
In this mosaic of life, we play our part.

Quiet Reverence

In stillness we gather, hearts open wide,
Amid nature's beauty, in silence, we bide.
Each rustling leaf speaks a language so true,
In quiet reverence, we find the new.

The soft glow of dawn breaks the night's hold,
Gifting us wisdom in hues of gold.
With every heartbeat, creation portrayed,
In quiet reverence, our fears start to fade.

The whispering winds carry sacred prayers,
Gentle reminders that life always cares.
In moments of stillness, the spirit expands,
Quiet reverence binding our hands.

As shadows grow long with the setting sun,
We find in the silence, our battles are won.
For peace that surpasses all words can impart,
In quiet reverence, we listen with heart.

So let us embrace this treasured creation,
In every heartbeat, a quiet foundation.
For in the silence, we hear heaven's call,
In quiet reverence, we rise, we do not fall.

Sacred Steps

Each step we take on this journey of grace,
Carries the weight of the sacred space.
With every heartbeat, a promise unfolds,
In sacred steps, our spirit consoles.

The path is winding, with blessings to find,
Lessons of patience, in nature outlined.
With faith as our compass, we walk hand in hand,
Sacred steps guiding us, through this land.

The mountains may rise with a challenge to face,
But with courage and love, we quicken our pace.
With eyes to the heavens, we rise from the ground,
In sacred steps, our purpose is found.

Footprints in sand, or tracks in the mud,
Marking the journey, a life drenched in blood.
But joy is the essence; we shall not despair,
Sacred steps lead us to moments so rare.

So in every challenge, let us dance, let us leap,
For under the stars, our dreams we shall keep.
In the sacred of steps, our lives intertwine,
Together we walk, in this grand design.

Pilgrimage of the Soul

With every dawn, my heart does seek,
A path of light, though shadows speak.
In sacred whispers, I find my way,
Guided by grace through night and day.

The mountains high, the valleys low,
Each step I take, in faith I grow.
With burdens lightened, spirits soar,
In unity with the mercy's core.

A journey vast, where trials press,
Yet in the struggle, find my rest.
The flame of love, a beacon bright,
Leading me onward, into the light.

Through storms that rage, and winds that howl,
I march with purpose, a faithful owl.
In each dark moment, hope ignites,
Illuminating my endless nights.

At journey's end, when peace draws near,
I'll offer thanks, my soul sincere.
For in the pilgrimage, I've been made whole,
Transformed by love, the way of the soul.

Celestial Encumbrances

Beneath the heavens, I seek my fate,
Stars like candles, they illuminate.
With every burden, a lesson learned,
In shadows deep, the heart has turned.

A galaxy spins, reflecting grace,
In cosmic dance, I find my place.
Each heavenly body, a sage's word,
In silence vast, my soul has stirred.

Encumbered oft by doubt and fear,
Yet in the stillness, I draw near.
Divine connection wraps around,
In faith and hope, my heart is found.

Celestial whispers guide the way,
In twilight's hour, the shadows play.
Through burdens heavy, I feel the lift,
In sacred moments, I learn the gift.

So let the cosmos show its might,
As I navigate this sacred flight.
With every star, a promise known,
In celestial embrace, I am home.

Pilgrimage of the Soul

With every dawn, my heart does seek,
A path of light, though shadows speak.
In sacred whispers, I find my way,
Guided by grace through night and day.

The mountains high, the valleys low,
Each step I take, in faith I grow.
With burdens lightened, spirits soar,
In unity with the mercy's core.

A journey vast, where trials press,
Yet in the struggle, find my rest.
The flame of love, a beacon bright,
Leading me onward, into the light.

Through storms that rage, and winds that howl,
I march with purpose, a faithful owl.
In each dark moment, hope ignites,
Illuminating my endless nights.

At journey's end, when peace draws near,
I'll offer thanks, my soul sincere.
For in the pilgrimage, I've been made whole,
Transformed by love, the way of the soul.

Celestial Encumbrances

Beneath the heavens, I seek my fate,
Stars like candles, they illuminate.
With every burden, a lesson learned,
In shadows deep, the heart has turned.

A galaxy spins, reflecting grace,
In cosmic dance, I find my place.
Each heavenly body, a sage's word,
In silence vast, my soul has stirred.

Encumbered oft by doubt and fear,
Yet in the stillness, I draw near.
Divine connection wraps around,
In faith and hope, my heart is found.

Celestial whispers guide the way,
In twilight's hour, the shadows play.
Through burdens heavy, I feel the lift,
In sacred moments, I learn the gift.

So let the cosmos show its might,
As I navigate this sacred flight.
With every star, a promise known,
In celestial embrace, I am home.

Anointed Pack

In fellowship, we walk this road,
Anointed hearts, a shared abode.
Together strong, when dark days come,
With steadfast faith, we overcome.

By grace we rise, and love we share,
Each sacred bond, a crown of care.
In every struggle, side by side,
Anointed pack, we shall abide.

The journey long, with tears and toil,
Yet in unity, our spirits coil.
For in the trials, our hearts align,
In holy purpose, a love divine.

Through every storm, we praise and sing,
In trials faced, new hope we bring.
Together we stand, with arms held wide,
In the anointed, we shall confide.

A tapestry woven with threads of trust,
In every heart, the holy must.
As one we rise, united and true,
In the sacred pack, our spirits renew.

Threads of Hope

In woven fabric, our stories blend,
Each thread a promise, a hand to lend.
Through trials faced, a tapestry grows,
In every stitch, a tale of prose.

The light of dawn breaks through the night,
In threads of hope, we weave our light.
With every heartbeat, we stand as one,
In love's embrace, our fears undone.

Gather my kind, from far and near,
In the web of faith, we persevere.
Through life's design, both straight and curved,
In sacred threads, the love observed.

From pain arises strength anew,
In every thread, the path shines through.
Though frayed at times, we mend with grace,
In hope's embrace, we'll find our place.

So let us cherish each woven seam,
In life's great quilt, we are the dream.
For in these threads, our spirits cope,
Together we rise, in threads of hope.

Pilgrim's Plea at the Crossroads

At the crossroads I stand, in my heart a plea,
Guide my weary feet, O Lord, follow Thee.
Whispers of the past, in shadows they creep,
I seek Your guidance, in faith I shall leap.

Through trials of spirit, through valleys of doubt,
Your light will illuminate paths to shout.
With every step forward, my burdens aflame,
I rise in Your name, and call out, 'I came.'

Oh, journey divine, wrap me in grace,
In each turning moment, behold Your face.
As I tread this road, with purpose anew,
O sovereign guide, my heart beats for You.

When shadows encumber, and fears come to call,
I'll lean on Your promise, I'll rise and not fall.
With faith as my armor, and hope in my song,
To the crossroads I journey, to where I belong.

Covenant of the Encumbered

In shadows of silence, I weave my lament,
A covenant forged, in trials well spent.
The weight of my sorrow, like stones on my chest,
Yet deep in Your presence, I find my rest.

Each burden I carry, You carry with me,
We journey together, my soul set free.
In prayers of the broken, my spirit finds peace,
Your love cloaks my heart, granting sweet release.

The chains that once bound me, begin to fall away,
In the warmth of Your mercy, I greet each new day.
With hands raised to heaven, I sing my refrain,
In the covenant made, I'm reborn again.

Though storms may encircle, and darkness may loom,
Your presence, my shelter, dispels every gloom.
Together we traverse this winding road's grace,
In the covenant binding, I find my true place.

Vows Under a Starlit Burden

Beneath the vast heavens, our vows we declare,
With starlight as witness, we lay our hearts bare.
In the hush of the night, our dreams intertwine,
Carved into the sky, Your whisper divine.

The burdens we carry, though heavy with tears,
Are lifted in union, dissolving our fears.
In the dance of the cosmos, our spirits align,
Bound by holy promises, forever entwined.

Guided by starlight, through shadows we tread,
Each step is a promise, where angels have led.
Your love is the lantern that brightens my way,
In the solace of night, together we stay.

As the heavens above, they sing out our song,
We forge on together, where we both belong.
With faith as our compass and hope as our guide,
Under starlit burdens, in You we confide.

Tribulations as Tapestries of Hope

In the loom of my spirit, threads interlace,
Each tribulation a part of Your grace.
Through trials and heartaches, where shadows may creep,

You weave me together, Your promises keep.

The colors of struggle, they brighten the thread,
Through tapestry woven, I rise from the dead.
Each knot tells a story, of courage displayed,
In the fabric of love, Your truth is arrayed.

With faith as my needle, and prayers as my loom,
I craft from the darkness, a vibrant new bloom.
Each moment of anguish, each sigh from the soul,
Becomes a sweet melody, a part of the whole.

So here in the weft, I see clearer each day,
These tribulations, though heavy, convey.
In the tapestry's beauty, I find as I cope,
In the tears and the laughter, I fashion my hope.

Milton Keynes UK
Ingram Content Group UK Ltd.
UKHW020039271124
451585UK00012B/945

9 789916 899403